My Shadow

Written by Rachel Mitchell
Illustrated by Nancy Carpenter

My shadow moves when I do.

When I move away, it grows big.

When I move close, it gets small.

When I go up the stairs, my shadow goes up the stairs, too.

When I play the drum, my shadow plays the drum, too.

My shadow can also make shapes.

My shadow can be a snail.

My shadow can be a whale.

My shadow can be a spaceship
or a plane.

My shadow can be a frog or a train.

My shadow can be a crown or a tree.

My shadow can be a chick or a monkey.

My shadow can be a flag or a shark.

But my shadow can never be . . .

in the dark.